Learn to Play
Piano / Keyboard
With
Filo & Pastry

*A Beginners Book For Children &
Very Silly Adults!*

Martin Woodward

ISBN: 978-1-291-53010-0

Copyright © Martin Woodward 2013

All rights reserved

Printing for buyers use only is permitted

Enquires: http://gonkmusic.com

Acknowledgements

To all the fantastic musicians who I've had the privilege of working with back in the 1960s / 70s including: Pip Williams (guitarist / record producer); Tex Marsh (drummer); Roger Flavell (bassist); Kevin Fogarty (guitarist); Ralph Denyer (singer / songwriter); Phil Childs (bassist); Jim Smith (drums); George Lee (saxophonist).

To my early mentors: Alan Simonds (guitarist / vocalist); big bruv Steve (guitarist) and Mr. Henley (my inspirational music teacher at Warlingham School 1960 - 65).

And to Myriad Software: http://www.myriad-online.com for the Melody Assistant music notation software which was used for the production of this book. - Thanks!

Contents

Introduction 8

Keyboard Notes 10

Rhythm Part 1 14

The Grand Staff 18

    How the Notes Relate to the Keyboard 22

Let's Begin 24

    Correct Hand Positioning 25

    Back and Forth 1 26

    Back and Forth 2 27

    Stepping Stones 1 28

    Stepping Stones 2 29

    5 Finger Exercise 1 30

    5 Finger Exercise 2 31

Your First Test 33

Rhythm Part 2 36

    Tied Notes 38

    4/4 Timing 39

    2/4 Timing 40

    3/4/ Timing 41

    6/8 Timing 41

More Tunes & Exercises 43

    Staccato 43

    Fermata 43

Learn to Play Piano / Keyboard With Filo & Pastry - Copyright © Martin Woodward 2013 - www.gonkmusic.com

Repeat Bars	44
Sharps, Flats and Intervals	45
The Gonk March	47
Grubby Hands	48
Disaster Strikes	50
The Jolly Farmer	52
The Jolly Farmer - Attempt 2	53
Jolly Milkmaid	54
Ringo's Beetle Jig	56
Ringo's Beetle Jig (words)	57
The Clown Waltz	58
Two More finger exercises	60

Your Second Test **62**

Your First Scales **64**

Pre Scale Exercises	64
Passing the Thumb under (ascending)	64
Passing the 3rd Finger over (descending)	64
C Major Scale	66
G Major Scale	67
F Major Scale	68
Chromatic Scale	69
The Harmonic Minor Scale	70
A Minor (Harmonic) Scale	71
E Minor (Harmonic) Scale	72
D Minor (Harmonic) Scale	73

Test Answers **74**

Learn to Play Piano / Keyboard With Filo & Pastry - Copyright © Martin Woodward 2013 - www.gonkmusic.com

Test 1 Answers..*74*

Test 2 Answers..*74*

Sad Goodbyes & Download Link **76**

Further Reading..**77**

Introduction

Bonjour mon ami - that's French for 'Good day my friend'!

My name is Alan Duvet and as you can see, I am a Gonk - A French Gonk! - *The* French Connection Gonk! But don't let this put you off as I speak very good English and I'm a very friendly Gonk - like all Gonks!

I will be teaching you to play the piano or keyboard along with your fellow pupils Filo and Pastry the Number 1 almost identical Gonkling twins who you can see below.

Filo and Pastry will probably ask many of the questions that you may have. They also have grubby, sticky little fingers possibly just like you, but we will deal with this issue shortly!

If you're wondering which one is Filo and which one is Pastry - Filo is always on the left - which means that Pastry is always on the right!

Pastry also has a tattoo of a squashed gooseberry on his bum, but as this is a respectable book, we can't show you this.

I'd also like you to meet two of my helpers: Leeroy who deals with 'rhythm' and Angus McDangle who is the 'note keeper' - he keeps the notes in his cupboard ready for when we need them.

In case you haven't noticed they are Gonks also.

See if you can figure out which one is which!

If you haven't worked it out yet, Leeroy is the one with the woolly hat and Angus McDangle is the other one!

Keyboard Notes

Now the first thing that we're going to do is go on a hunting trip.

"Whoopee doo can I bring my fishing net?" - asks Pastry.

No, it's not that sort of hunting trip. We're going to go hunting for the most important note on the keyboard which is Middle 'C'.

Now keyboards and pianos come in all different shapes and sizes. Some have got lots of keys and some not so many, but all have the same basic arrangement of black and white notes. For our purposes here, it makes no difference whether you have a big one or a little one!

If you look closely you will see that the black notes are in groups of two then three.

This enables us to find every single note easily. And the first one that you must learn is 'C' which can be found just to the left of two black keys.

"I can find lots of them", says Filo, "so which one is 'C'?"

That's very observant of you Gonkling, and the answer is that they are all 'C', but each one is an octave apart. And if you count up from one C to the next, you'll find that they're eight white notes apart. That's why it's called an octave, just like an 'octopus' is called that because it has eight legs, and an octagon because it has eight sides and an octet being a group of eight.

"And like October is the 10th month", says Filo with a cheeky smirk.

Very clever Gonkling! - But in the original Roman Gonk calendar October *was* the eighth month.

2 Octaves C - C **1 Octave C - C**

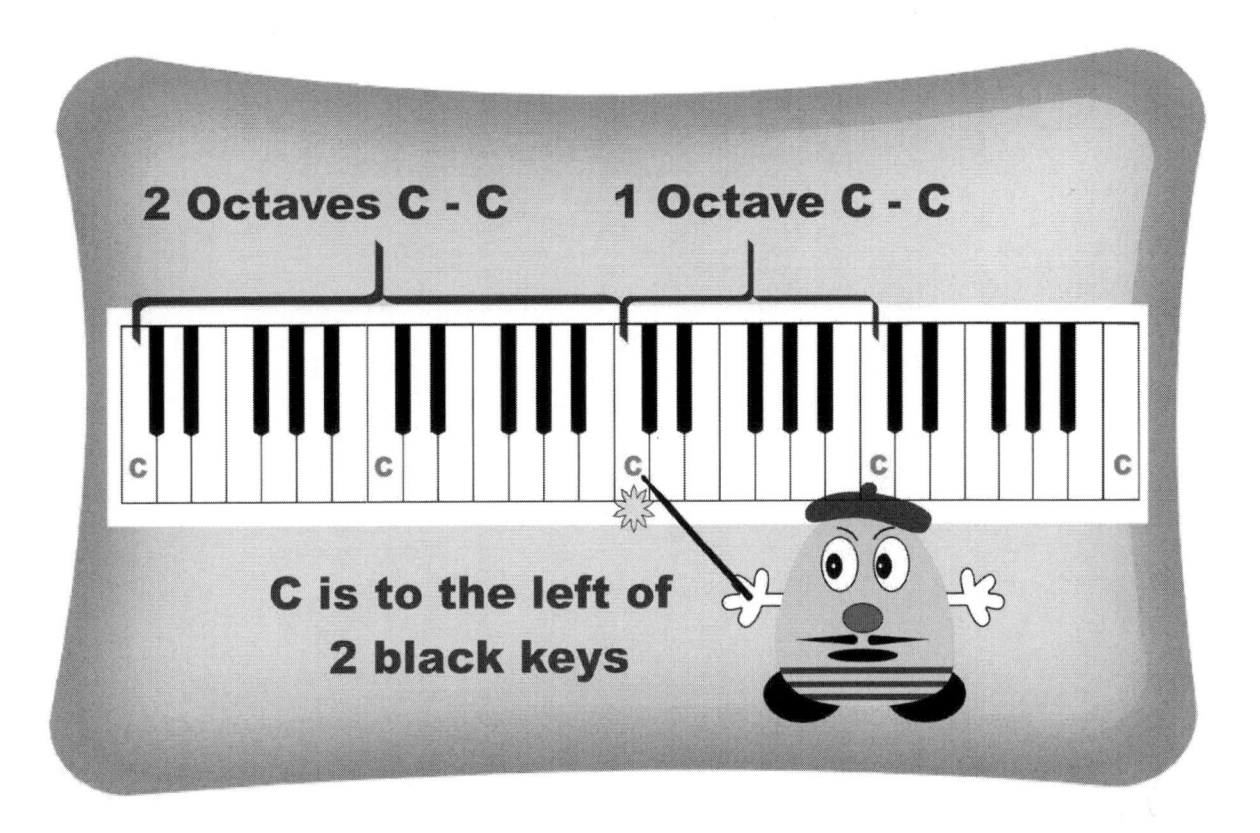

C is to the left of 2 black keys

But 'middle C' is the 'C' that is more or less in the middle of the keyboard and because it is so important, we are going to put a star on ours as shown.

Now all the notes to the left of middle C get gradually lower in pitch and all the notes to the right gradually get higher. And usually you will use your right hand for the higher notes and your left hand for the lower notes. That is unless you are standing on your head in which case it's the other way round!

"So which hand plays middle C?"

That's a good question Gonkling and the answer is that it could be either, but I will explain more shortly.

"And what about all the other notes?"

Don't worry I haven't forgotten them, but next you need to understand your finger numbering in relation to music.

As far as music is concerned what most people will call their 'first' finger is their 'second' finger as in music the 'first' finger is always your thumb.

Learn to Play Piano / Keyboard With Filo & Pastry - Copyright © Martin Woodward 2013 - www.gonkmusic.com

Hands with Palms up

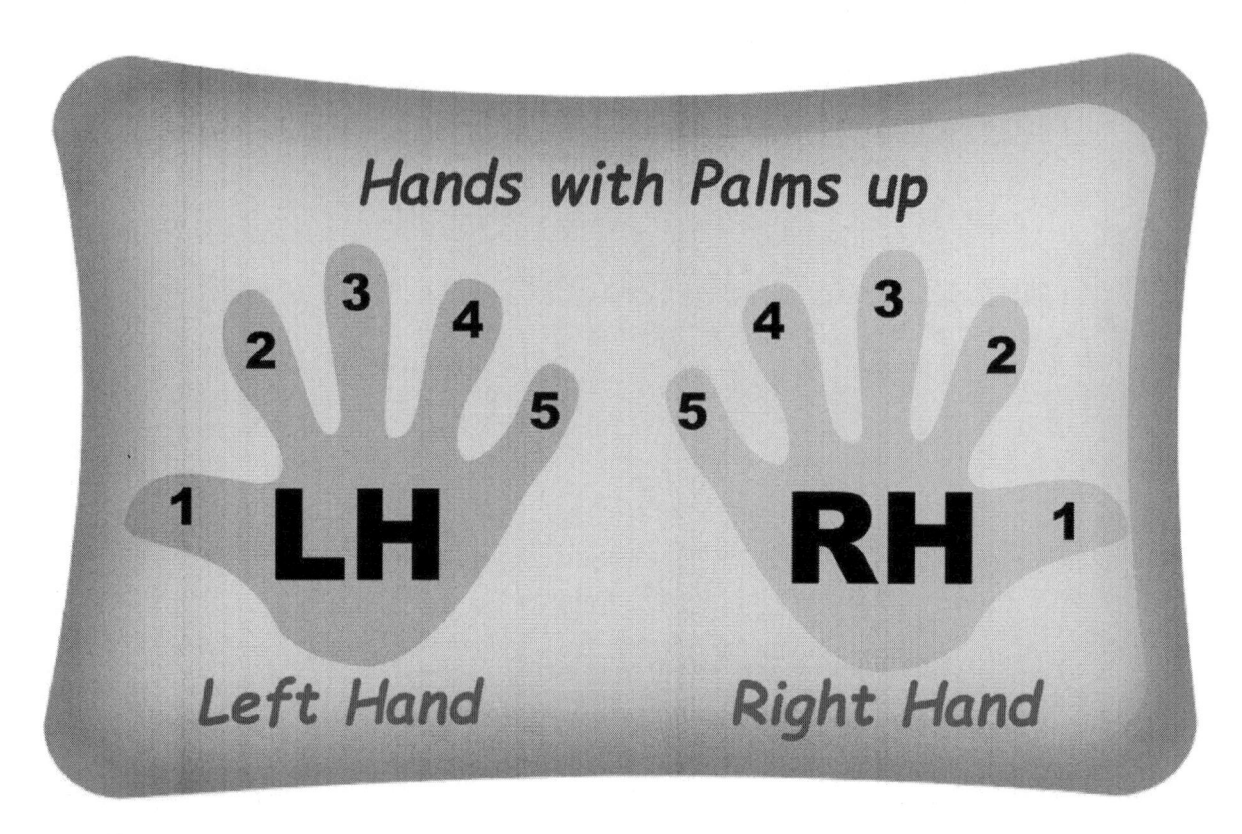

LH — Left Hand (fingers: 1, 2, 3, 4, 5)
RH — Right Hand (fingers: 1, 2, 3, 4, 5)

"But Gonks only have four fingers on each hand!"

I know, but most of the other girls and boys have five and anyway Gonks have an extra 'magic' finger that no-one else knows about, so don't go spreading this about.

Ok Gonklings, now I'll show you what all the other notes are called, but I don't want you to get too confused about all this at the moment. We will be taking it all step by step.

Here's the other notes!

C D E F G A B C D E F G A B C D E F G A B C D E F G A B C D E F G A B C

"What about the black ones, what are they called?"

We'll deal with those a little later as we need to, but you have plenty to learn for the time being.

And next you need to learn a little bit about rhythm from Leeroy the Drummer Gonk.

"Thank you M. Duvet."

Rhythm Part 1

Right Gonklings, now we're going to learn a little about note values and rhythm.

There's quite a few different note values, but the three that we are going to learn today are:

- Semibreve which = 4 beats (often referred to as a whole note)
- Minim which = 2 beats and
- Crotchet which = 1 beat (often referred to as a quarter note)

Now Gonklings, can you count up to four?

"Of course I can, I can count up to ten!" - says Filo proudly.

Well that's great because in music you will rarely need to count more than eight.

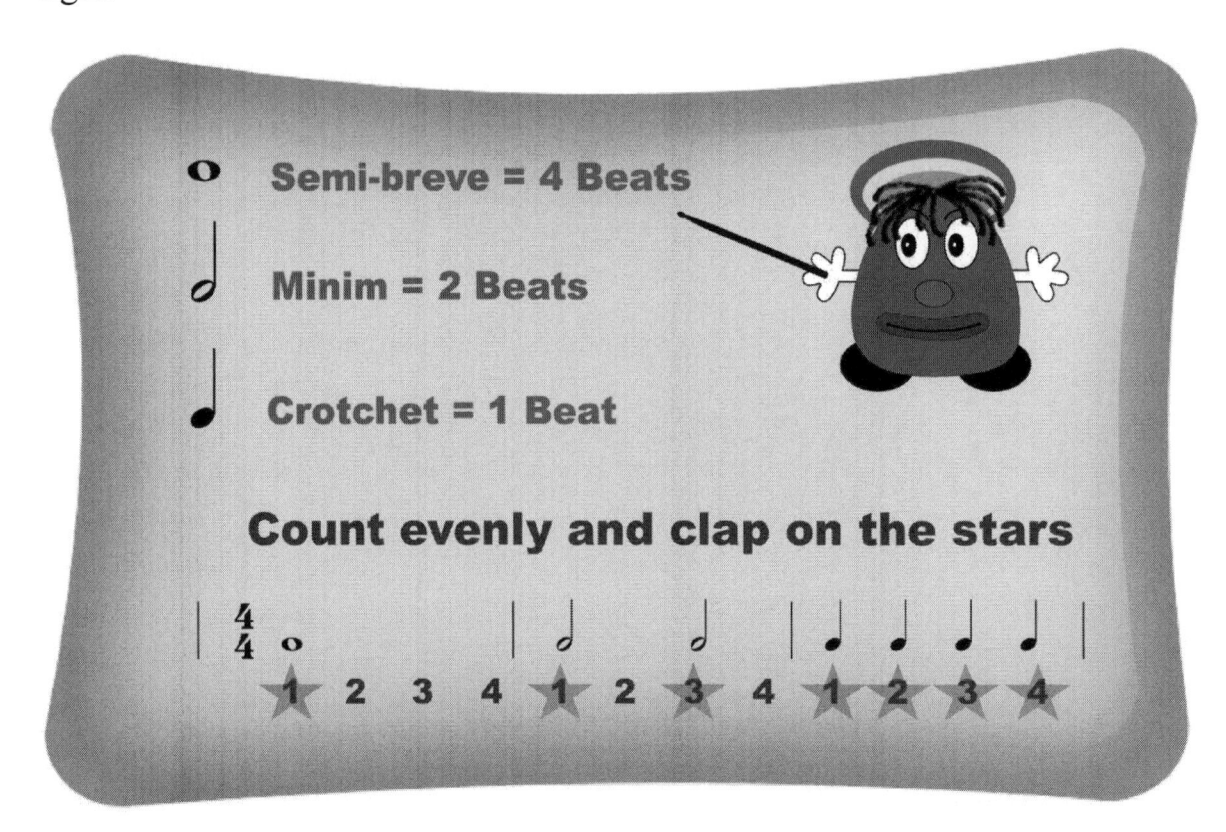

Semi-breve = 4 Beats

Minim = 2 Beats

Crotchet = 1 Beat

Count evenly and clap on the stars

Now I want you to count out loud or in your head: **1 - 2 - 3 - 4 - 1 - 2 - 3 - 4 - 1 - 2 - 3 - 4** and clap your hands on the beats with the stars. Then you'll be clapping the rhythm.

Notice the **4/4** sign at the beginning. This means that there are 4 beats to each bar, which is why you are counting to 4. You can see the **'bar lines'** above between each 4 beats.

Now here's a couple more to try before we move on.

Here's Some More!

Count evenly and clap on the stars

Now every **4/4** bar must always add up to four beats, that is either 4 crotchets, or 2 minims, or 2 crotchets and a minim etc. There can't be any 'leftovers'.

So if we need a gap between notes, that is a brief moment of silence, we have to add a 'rest' to make up the correct value.

So there are 'rests' to the same value of every 'note'.

Rests

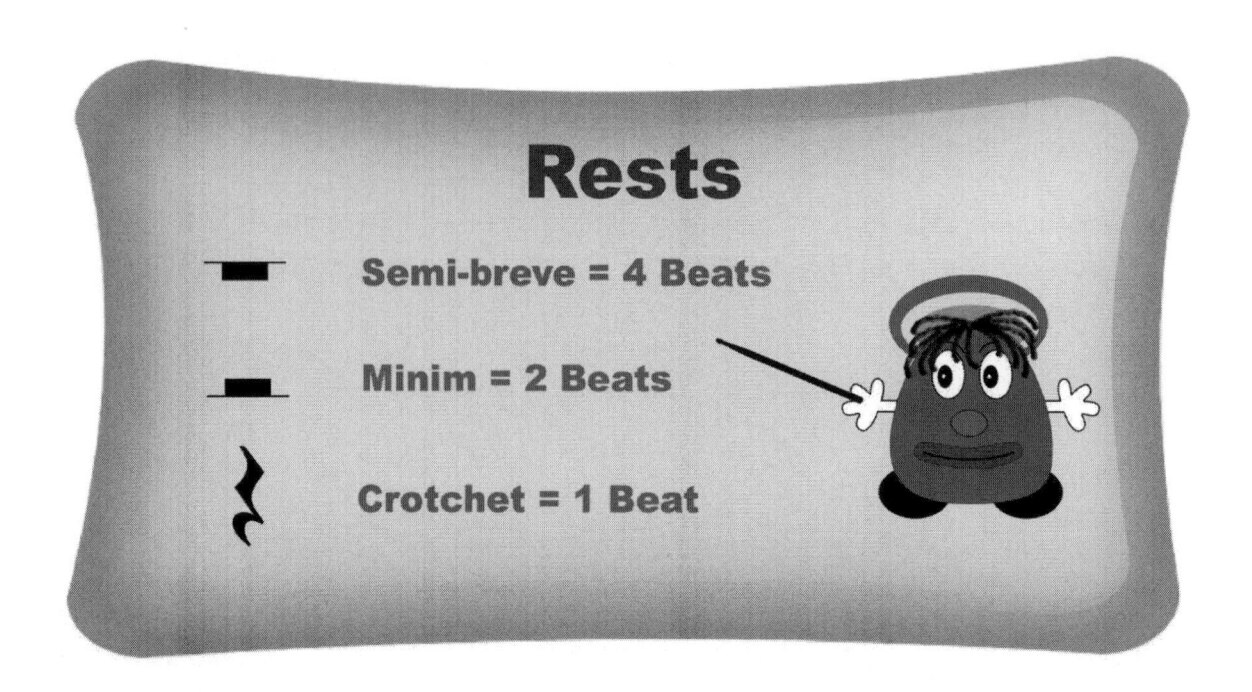

- Semi-breve = 4 Beats
- Minim = 2 Beats
- Crotchet = 1 Beat

The Semibreve and minim rests look very similar but actually are rarely confused as the semibreve will take up a whole bar. And also remember that a minim 'rests' on the line and the semibreve 'hangs'!

Now let's have a look at how the rests fit in with the notes and do some more clapping.

Notice that the very last bar contains a semibreve rest so is totally silent.

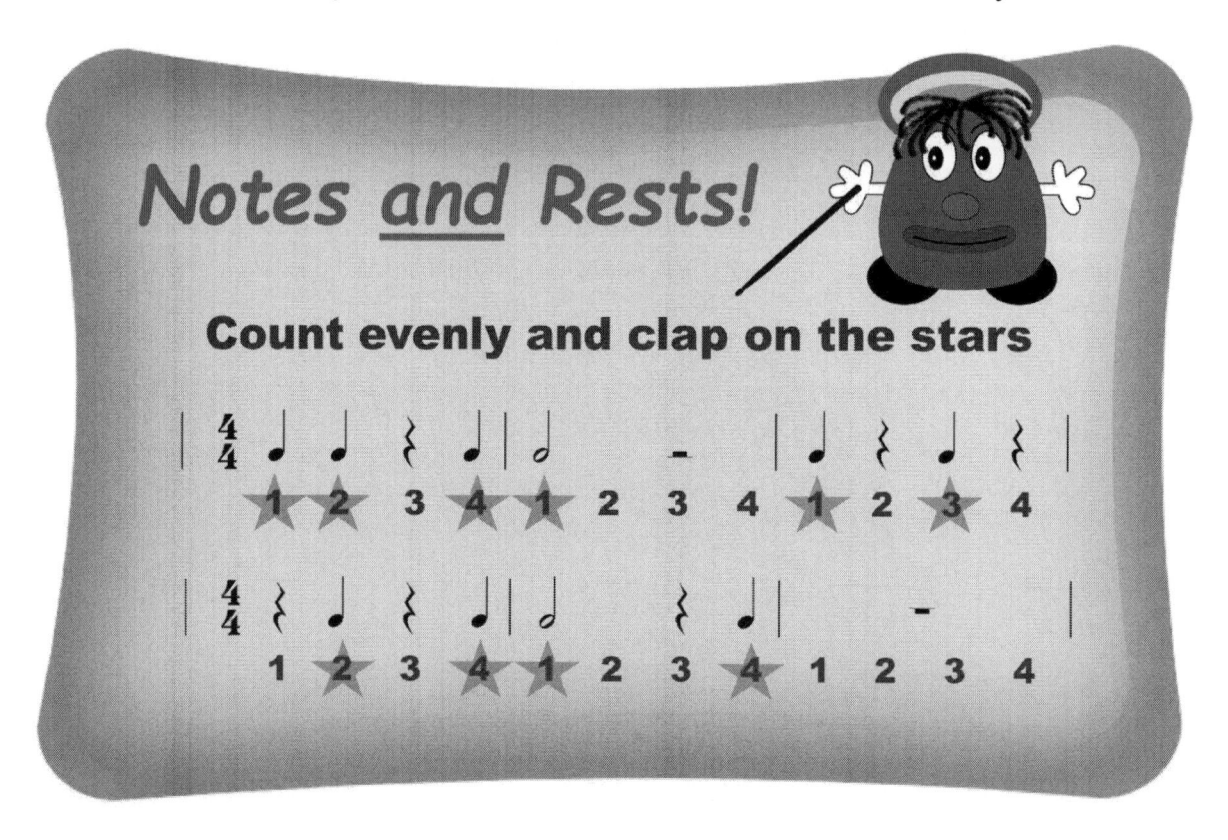

Notes and Rests!

Count evenly and clap on the stars

Ok Gonklings, that's it for rhythm for the time being, but there will be much more later.

"Thank you Leeroy!"

The Grand Staff

Thank you Leeroy. Now in order to see the notes of the keyboard in music notation, we need to look at the Grand Staff.

The Grand staff is made up of two 'staves' or 'staffs' of five lines each, the top one being the treble 'clef' which is mainly used for the higher notes by the right hand and the bass 'clef' mainly used for the lower notes by the left hand.

The Treble & Bass Clefs

This is the Treble clef symbol

And this is the Bass clef symbol

"What's the difference between a staff and a stave?"

Actually no-one seems to know for sure, but a staff *is* a stave - it's just a word, well two words actually, so don't worry about it!

The important thing that you need to learn is that the 'staves' or 'staffs' are split into the two clefs - these are what you need to learn and remember.

Learn to Play Piano / Keyboard With Filo & Pastry - Copyright © Martin Woodward 2013 - www.gonkmusic.com

The Grand Staff

Notes of the Treble Clef

F A C E E G B D F

A C E G G B D F A

Notes of the Bass Clef

An easy way to remember the notes is to think of them in sections like:

- Treble Clef *space* notes **F A C E** - the word *FACE!*
- Treble Clef *line* notes **E G B D F** - *Every Good Boy Deserves Favours!*
- Bass Clef *space* notes **A C E G** - *All Cows Eat Grass!*
- Bass Clef *line* notes **G B D F A** - *Giant Bears Don't Fly Aeroplanes!*

"Yes, but mummy whales are called cows and they don't eat grass!"

Very true Gonkling, but let's just say that *nearly* all cows eat grass!

"So which one is 'middle C'?"

Well actually 'middle C' is not in the above illustration, because it falls below the lines of the treble clef and above the lines of the bass clef. In fact it's exactly mid way between both clefs.

The next illustration will show you where it is!

Learn to Play Piano / Keyboard With Filo & Pastry - Copyright © Martin Woodward 2013 - www.gonkmusic.com

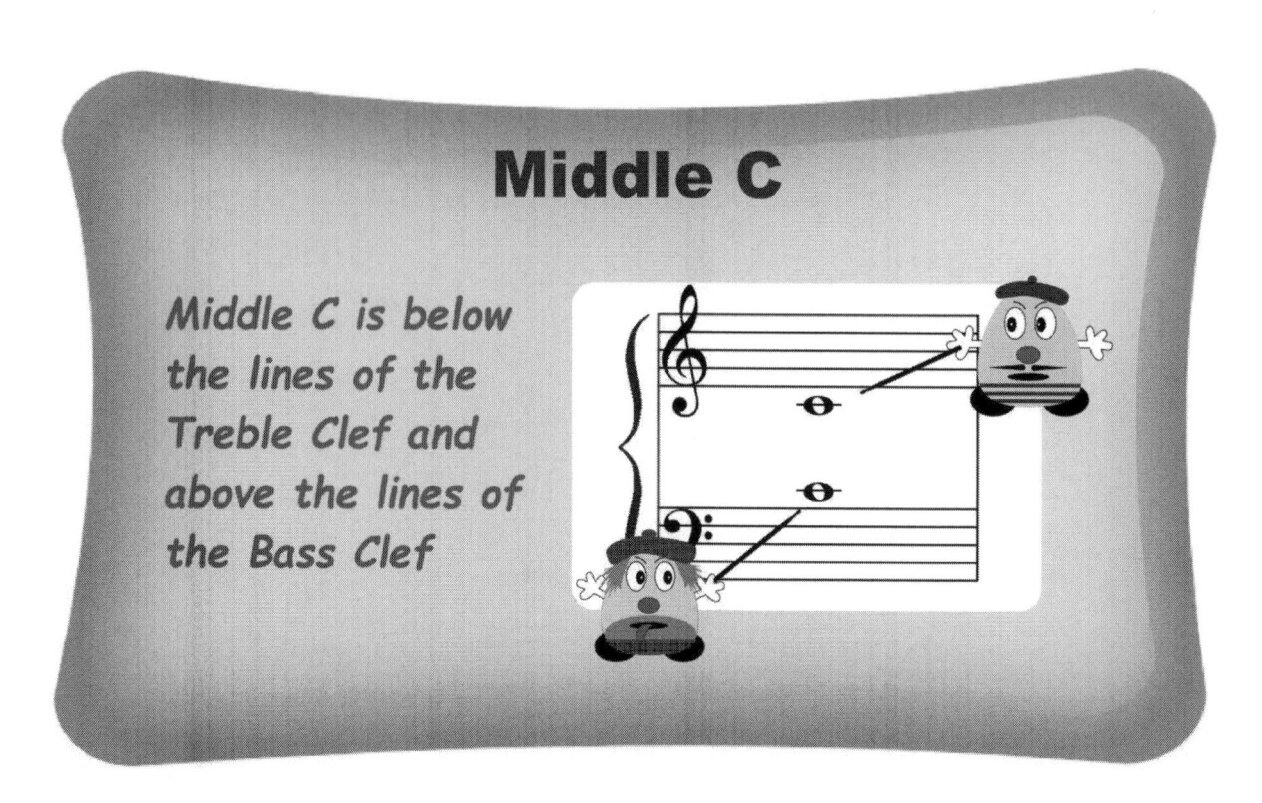

Middle C

Middle C is below the lines of the Treble Clef and above the lines of the Bass Clef

If we bring the two clefs closer together, you will see that there is an imaginary line exactly midway between the two clefs and this is where middle C lives.

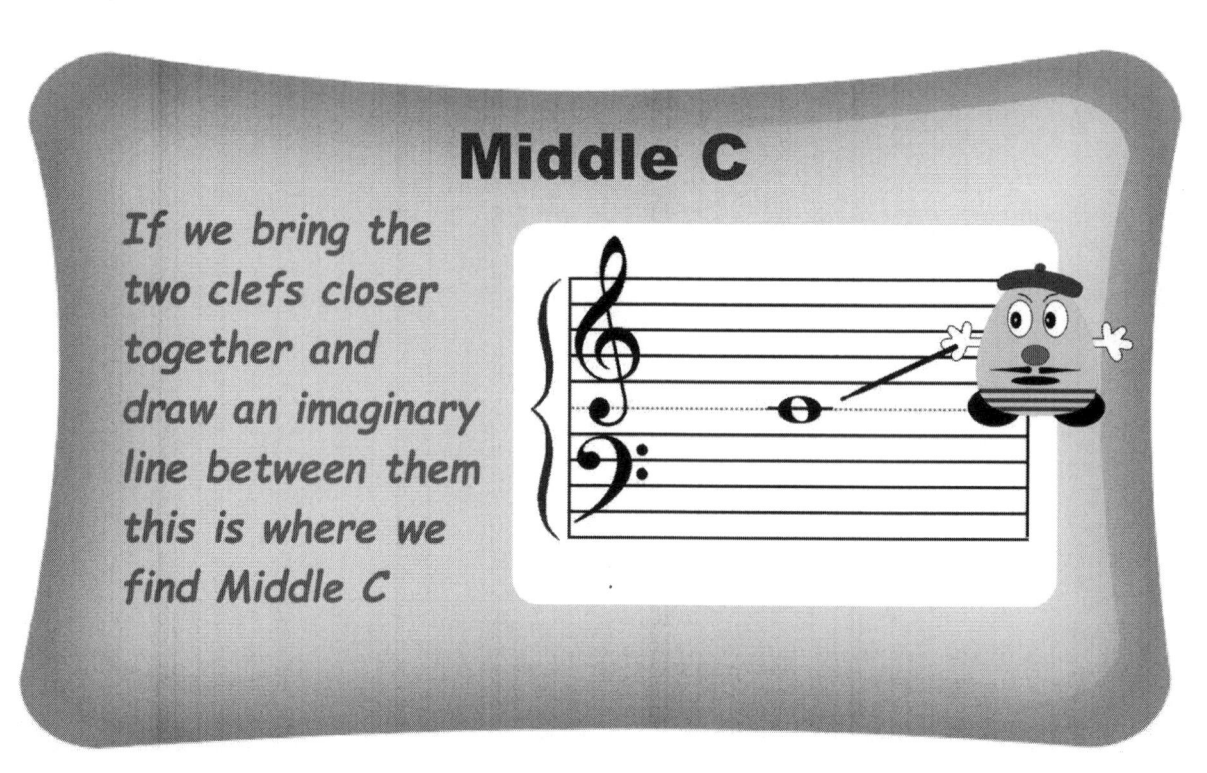

Middle C

If we bring the two clefs closer together and draw an imaginary line between them this is where we find Middle C

And this is why middle C has a line drawn through the middle of it. This is called a ledger line and happens with some other notes as well, in fact any time a note goes above or below the clef lines.

Now the notes both sides of middle C (B and D) also fall either above or below the staff lines which can be seen next.

Learn to Play Piano / Keyboard With Filo & Pastry - Copyright © Martin Woodward 2013 - www.gonkmusic.com

Other Notes Between the Staffs

The notes shown here are the same notes written in different clefs!

Notes Above or Below the Staves

Some notes go above or below the staff lines as shown here!

The two C's shown here are 4 octaves apart!

Now there are also notes that are both above the treble clef and below the bass clef.

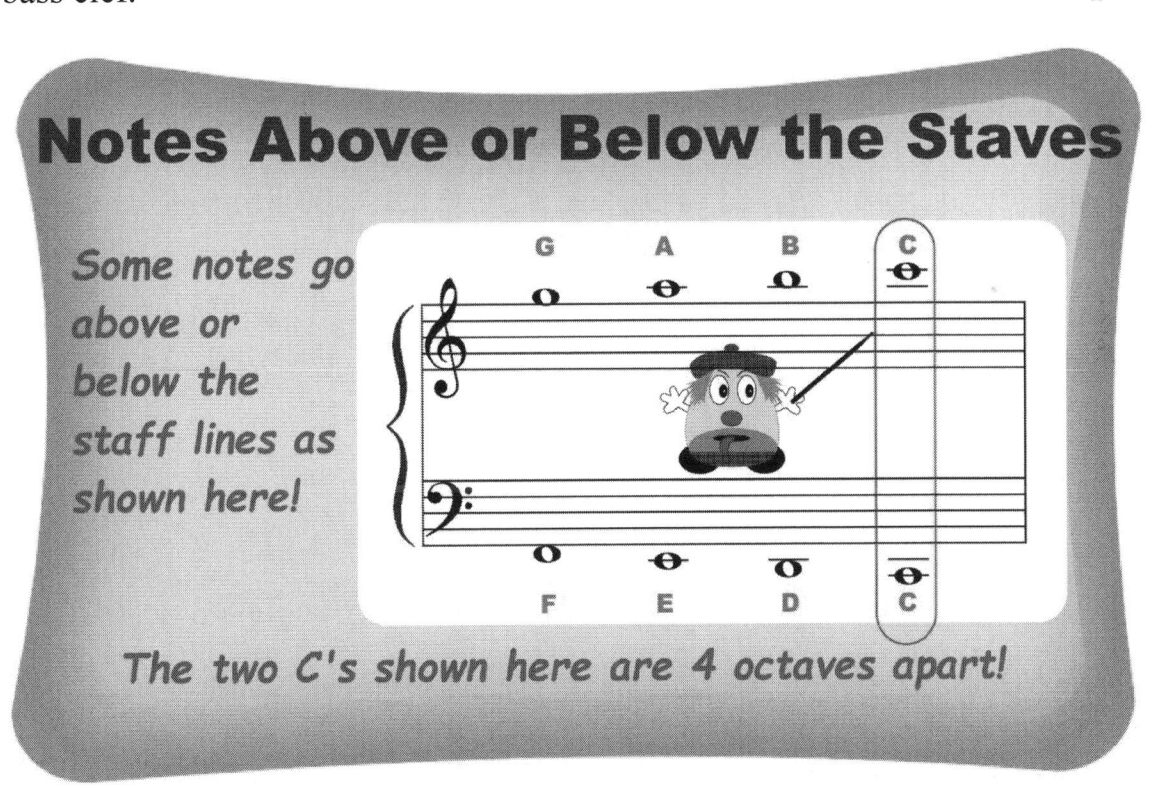

"Oh this is too confusing for a little Gonkling like me M. Duvet, I don't think I'll ever understand all this!" - says Pastry.

Please don't distress yourself Gonklings, we will be dealing with the notes one step at a time and it will all become clear as we progress.

Learn to Play Piano / Keyboard With Filo & Pastry - Copyright © Martin Woodward 2013 - www.gonkmusic.com

How the Notes Relate to the Keyboard

Now we'll look at how the musical notes relate to the keyboard.

This next diagram may look a little confusing and difficult to read, and if you are reading this on a tablet, it may not be clear.

Notes of Both Clefs

Middle C and its neighbours are shown in both clefs!

To make this easier to see, below I have split the keyboard into two 2 octave sections, one for each clef, but remember that we have put a star on Middle C so that you can always find it!

So notice that the next two diagrams are actually the same as the above diagram split into two.

It may be useful for you to print out these three diagrams and look at them in detail.

"Ay and don't forget that poor old Angus McDangle has been up all night making these diagrams! .... And that's why I didn't even have time to shave this morning!"

"Oh, thank you Angus, we really appreciate it!"

Learn to Play Piano / Keyboard With Filo & Pastry - Copyright © Martin Woodward 2013 - www.gonkmusic.com

Notes of the 𝄞 Treble Clef

Upper portion of keyboard

B C D E F G A B C D E F G A B C

Notes of the 𝄢 Bass Clef

Lower portion of keyboard

C D E F G A B C D E F G A B C D

Learn to Play Piano / Keyboard With Filo & Pastry - Copyright © Martin Woodward 2013 - www.gonkmusic.com

Let's Begin

Right Gonklings now we're ready to actually start working on the keyboard, but first let me check your grubby little hands!

"We've just washed them M. Duvet - honest!"

Was that before or after I saw you gonkhandling that slimy frog?

Let me have a look, hmmm, I don't want marmalade or decomposing frogs spawn all over my keyboard! .... Ok, that'll do for now, but rest assured I'll keep checking!

"I've still got him in my pocket," - whispers Pastry to Filo.

"Well don't let M. Duvet see him, remember he's French and they eat frogs legs there!"

What are you two Gonklings whispering about?

"Nothing M. Duvet!"

Did I hear one of you croak?

"It must have been the creaky chair M. Duvet!"

Hmmm......!

Correct Hand Positioning

Ok, having made sure that your hands are clean, the next thing is that you must be sure that you adopt a correct seating position so that you can achieve the correct hand position.

If your seating is incorrect (too low or too high) then your hand positioning will never be correct. And if they are too sticky you won't be able to let go of the keys!

The next pictures illustrate the correct and incorrect hand positions.

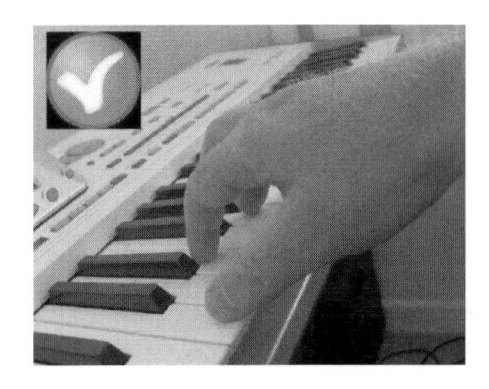

"Who's hairy hand is that it in the picture M. Duvet?"

That is 'Boiler Suit Bill' the roadie. I had to use his hand so that I could take the photos!

Back and Forth 1

Ok, our first piece is very simple and only requires the thumb on each hand.

But just because it's simple doesn't mean that you should rush it. You must pay attention to correct timing. And each note should be played evenly with equal pressure and held / released at the correct time.

Before you begin, count **1 - 2 - 3 - 4** etc. evenly, then when you feel ready begin playing on the next '**1**' beat. When you get to the last note, don't release it until you have counted to '**4**'.

It may help you to sing along with the song as you play.

You can hear all of the songs and exercises in order via the website link which I'll give you later. Or go now to - http://gonkmusic.com/back_forth.html

Learn to Play Piano / Keyboard With Filo & Pastry - Copyright © Martin Woodward 2013 - www.gonkmusic.com

Back and Forth 2

This next short piece is unsurprisingly slightly more difficult as you will need two fingers on each hand and also two more notes.

Take note of the correct hand positioning as shown above and begin to press the second key *as* you are releasing the first which will create a smooth transition which is known as **'legato'**.

Note that in this case 'middle C' is played by both hands (alternately) and the rhythm and rests are exactly the same as the last piece. Most importantly do not play any faster than you can manage. Speed is not important, but accuracy and steady timing is. ♫ http://gonkmusic.com/back_forth.html

---

Learn to Play Piano / Keyboard With Filo & Pastry - Copyright © Martin Woodward 2013 - www.gonkmusic.com

Stepping Stones 1

This next little piece introduces another note 'E' in the treble clef and the third finger of the right hand and fourth of the left hand.

And the C, B and G in the left hand are an octave lower than we used previously.

There are no rests in this piece, so each hand is a little more active.

You may need to practice each hand separately at first, which is fine on this piece as well as all the pieces to follow.

♪ http://gonkmusic.com/stepping_stones.html

Left foot right foot   here we go   on the step ping stones

Learn to Play Piano / Keyboard With Filo & Pastry - Copyright © Martin Woodward 2013 - www.gonkmusic.com

Stepping Stones 2

Now this is an extension of the last piece and adds two more new notes in the right hand - 'F' and 'G' along with the remaining fingers 4 & 5. And the new note 'A' in the left hand along with the 4th finger.

♪ http://gonkmusic.com/stepping_stones.html

5 Finger Exercise 1

Now Gonklings, the next two exercises are extremely important as they need every finger on each hand - even the magic Gonk finger. But as always practice these slowly and evenly.

We've also introduced some new notes as shown in the chart below.

In fact these are the notes of the C major scale (for two octaves) which we'll be talking about later. ♪ http://gonkmusic.com/5_finger.html

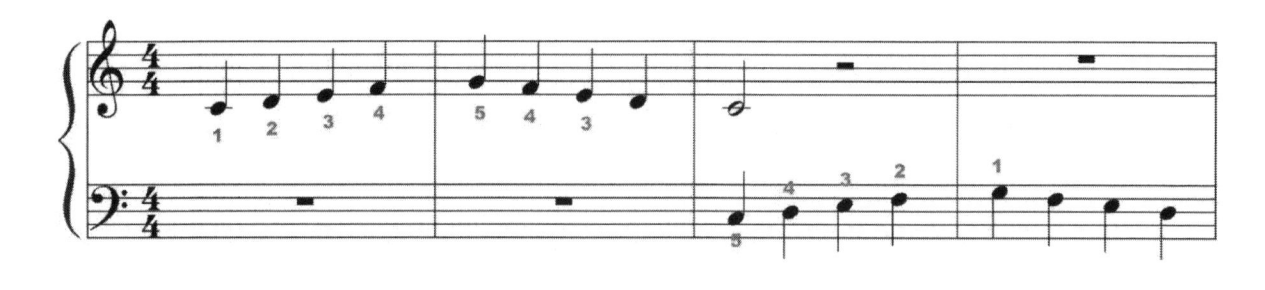

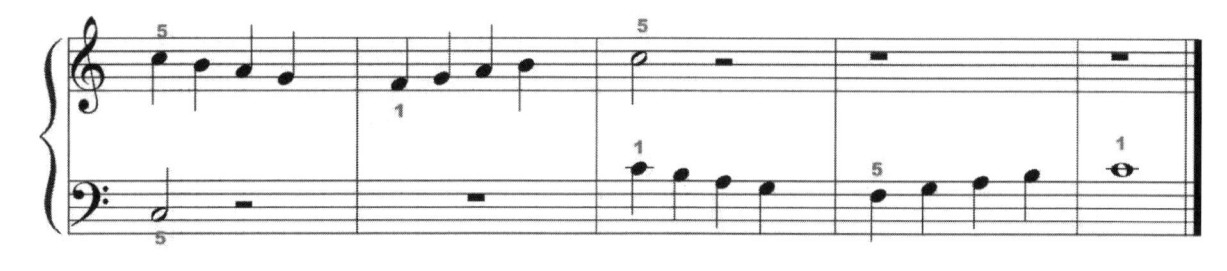

5 Finger Exercise 2

This next exercise is the without doubt the most difficult so far, but also the most important as it will help to give your fingers flexibility and independence.

Again you will need all your fingers and we have added just a couple more notes as shown - the top **'D's'** and bottom **'B's'**.

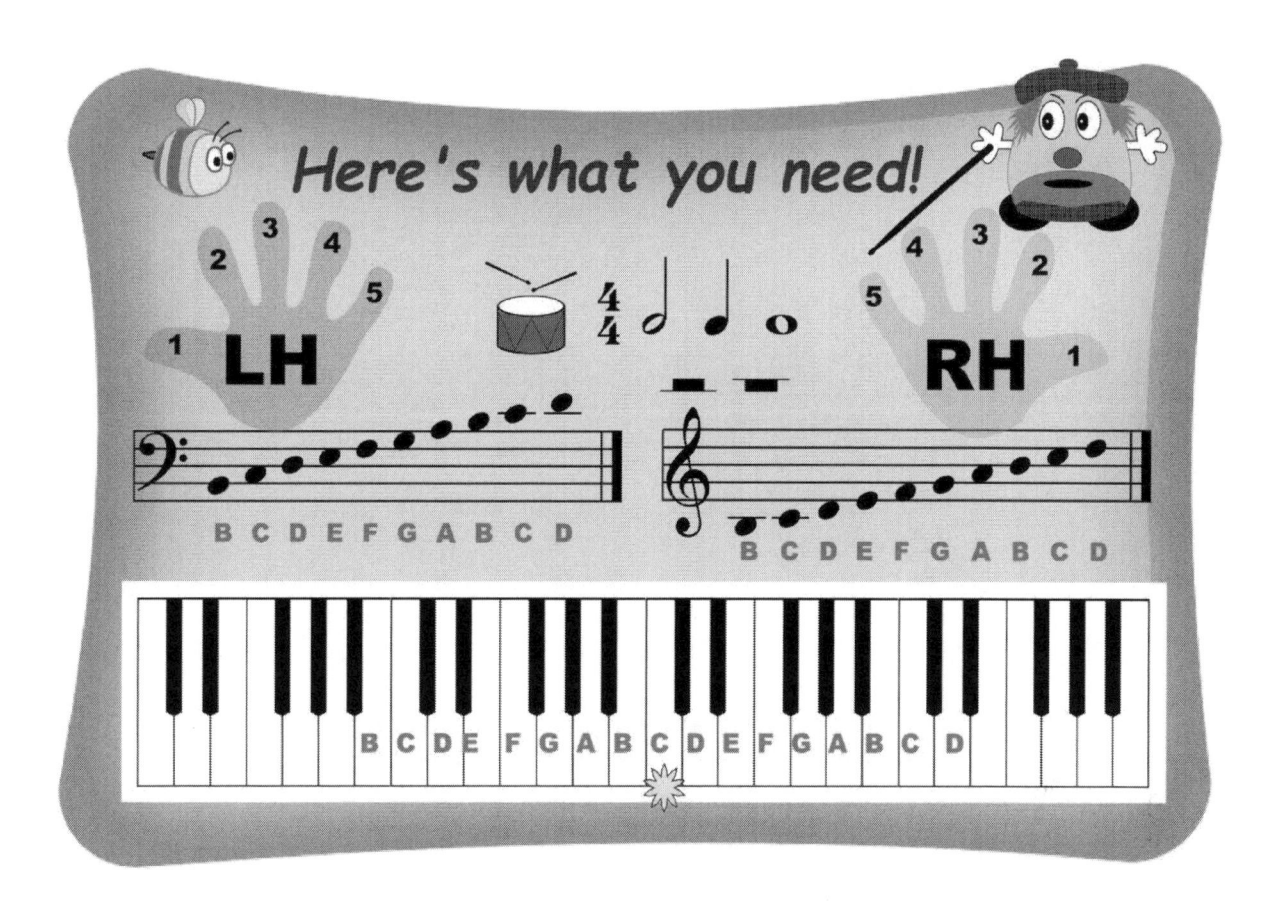

Look at the fingering carefully as at first it forms a pattern, but then alters slightly so that the new notes - the lower **'B's'** and top **'D's'** fit in.

"Oh we can see the pattern. You play a note, then miss a note then go back to the one that you missed!"

Yes, more or less Gonklings. The idea of this exercise is to 'separate' your fingers and not to just use them 'in order'. It's a very good exercise and well worth the effort, as you will see after only a few attempts.

"Yes, my fingers are working better already!" - says Filo.

🎵 http://gonkmusic.com/5_finger.html

Big Gonk Tip! - If you feel you need to, you can print out any or all of the exercises / tunes and write on the note names above or below each note.

Learn to Play Piano / Keyboard With Filo & Pastry - Copyright © Martin Woodward 2013 - www.gonkmusic.com

Your First Test

Now Gonklings it's time for your first test to see how much you understand of what we've covered so far.

"Oh please M. Duvet we are only little Gonklings and we don't like tests. Do we really have to do this?"

There is nothing to worry about Gonklings, the test is only to find out what you understand. And if you get any of the questions wrong, it only means that you will need to go back and have another look at what we've done so far.

You must understand that it's impossible to progress if you do understand correctly.

Ok, here we go.

Question 1

Looking at the keyboard chart shown here:

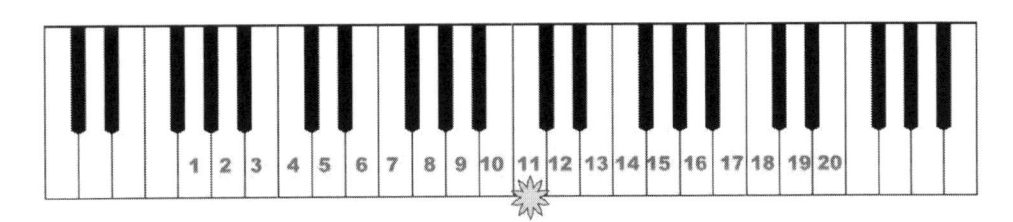

What are the notes called that are numbered:

    a) 11?

    b) 14?

    c) 9?

    d) 5?

    e) 13?

Question 2

Looking at the following diagram which is in the **treble** clef:

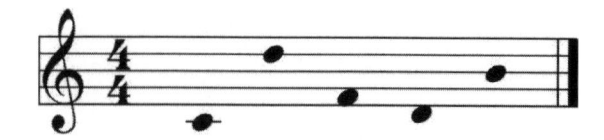

Identify the names of each note in order and show where they can be found on the keyboard in the first chart.

For instance the first note is 'C' and is No. 11 in the chart.

Question 3

Looking at the following diagram which is in the **bass** clef:

As before, identify the notes in order and where they can be found on the keyboard in the first chart.

Question 4

How many crotchets equal a minim?

Question 5

How many crotchets equal a semibreve?

Question 6

Is the following note a semibreve, minim or crotchet?

Question 7

Is the following note a semibreve, minim or crotchet?

Question 8

Is the following rest a semibreve, minim or crotchet?

𝄽

Question 9

How many minims could there be in a 4/4 bar?

Question 10

Which Gonk has a frog in his pocket?

"Oh M. Duvet that's not fair. How did you know that one of us has a frog in his pocket?"

Alan Duvet knows everything Gonklings. You cannot keep anything hidden from me. But don't worry, fortunately for your grotesque, slimy little friend, I do not eat frogs legs, nor am I ever likely to!

Anyway that's the end of your first little test. The correct answers can be found towards the end of the book.

If you have answered any questions incorrectly, you should look again at the information shown previously.

But do also remember that the most important aspect of playing the piano or keyboard is the actual physical practice, so please work hard at getting your fingers working well and pay attention to correct timing, accuracy and smoothness in your playing.

If you feel ready to proceed, we will now call on Leeroy again to explain some more about rhythm.

"Thank you M. Duvet and thank you Angus!"

Rhythm Part 2

Hello again Gonklings, now we're going to learn some more different note values to go with the ones we learnt earlier.

This will enable us to create far more interesting rhythms.

So just to re-cap so far we have covered:

- Semibreve which = 4 beats (often referred to as a whole note)
- Minim which = 2 beats
- Crotchet which = 1 beat (often referred to as a quarter note)
- Rests for all of the above and **4/4** timing.

"*Excuse me Leeroy, could you just explain again exactly what **4/4** timing means? - asks Filo.*

Certainly Gonkling, there's no point in continuing if you are not understanding properly.

The top '**4**' of the '**4/4**' symbol means that there are four beats to the bar and the bottom '**4**' tells us the value of the beats and as a crotchet is a quarter of a semibreve, this means that there are four quarter notes (crotchets) to each bar.

If the symbol was **2/4** this would that there would be two quarter notes (crotchets) to each bar and **3/4** would mean three crotchets to each bar.

And there are even more time signatures, which you will see shortly as we will be covering these today as well as some new note values.

The next note value that we are going to learn is the quaver which is half a crotchet. So two quavers = one crotchet. Sometime a quaver is known as an 'eighth' note as it is one eighth of a semibreve.

Adding this single time value alone will allow us to create many far more interesting rhythms.

Learn to Play Piano / Keyboard With Filo & Pastry - Copyright © Martin Woodward 2013 - www.gonkmusic.com

"Oh that's difficult Leeroy!"

Not really Gonkling, it just means that eight quavers equals one semibreve.

But also we are going to add 'dotted minims' and 'dotted crotchets'. Any note with a dot after it (not over) has its time value multiplied by a half.

So a dotted minim will equal **3** beats instead of **2** and a dotted crotchet will equal **1½** beats instead of **1**. And the same will apply to the dotted rests.

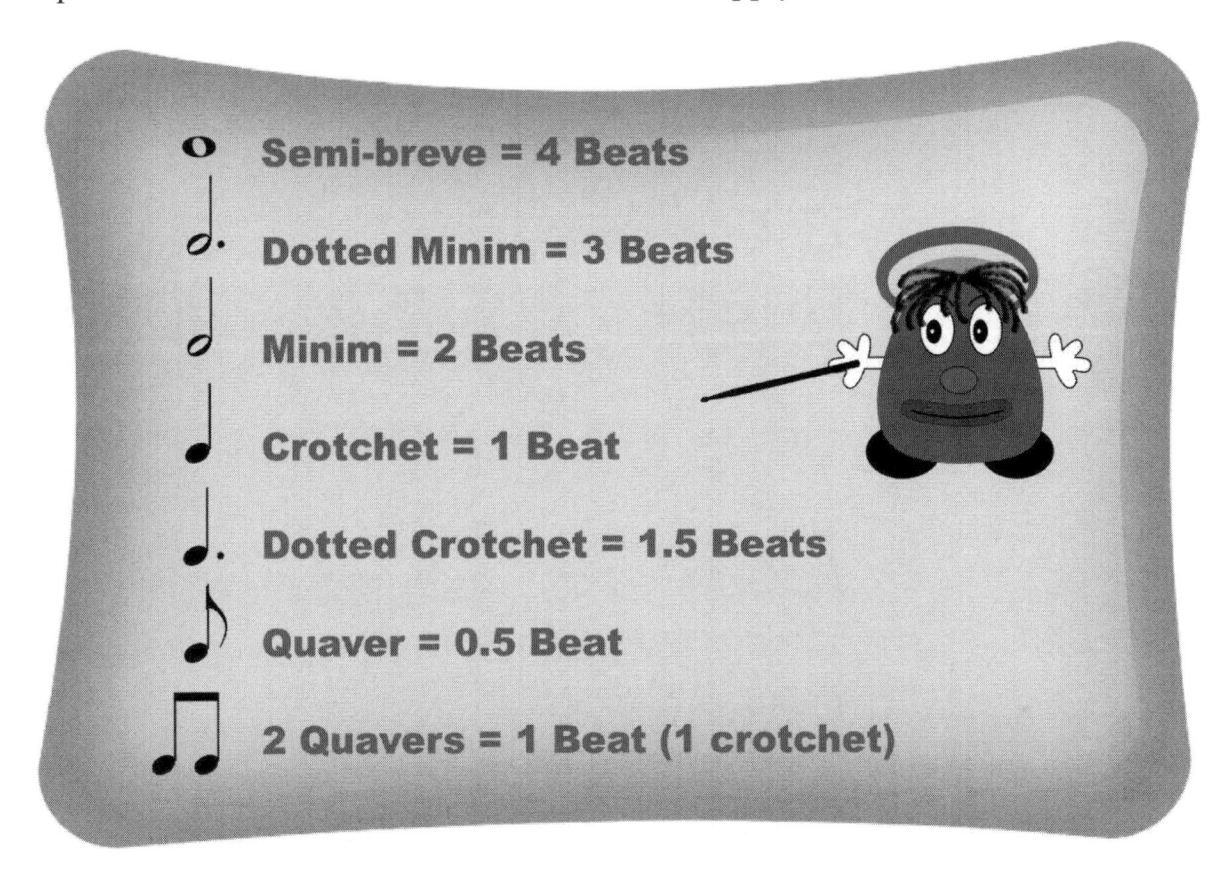

Semi-breve = 4 Beats

Dotted Minim = 3 Beats

Minim = 2 Beats

Crotchet = 1 Beat

Dotted Crotchet = 1.5 Beats

Quaver = 0.5 Beat

2 Quavers = 1 Beat (1 crotchet)

Note that a single quaver just has a tail, but when there are two or more together their tails are often joined as shown above.

"So what about dotted quavers?"

Yes Gonklings there are dotted quavers as well, which add half again onto their value, but to learn about those we'd also have to learn 'semi quavers' which have two tails instead of one. But we'll leave that for another time, as we have enough to deal with for the time being.

"And what about dotted rests?"

Learn to Play Piano / Keyboard With Filo & Pastry - Copyright © Martin Woodward 2013 - www.gonkmusic.com

Yes Gonklings there are dotted rests which work exactly the same. Although you will generally only find dotted minim rests in **12/8** timing. But I'll show you these now.

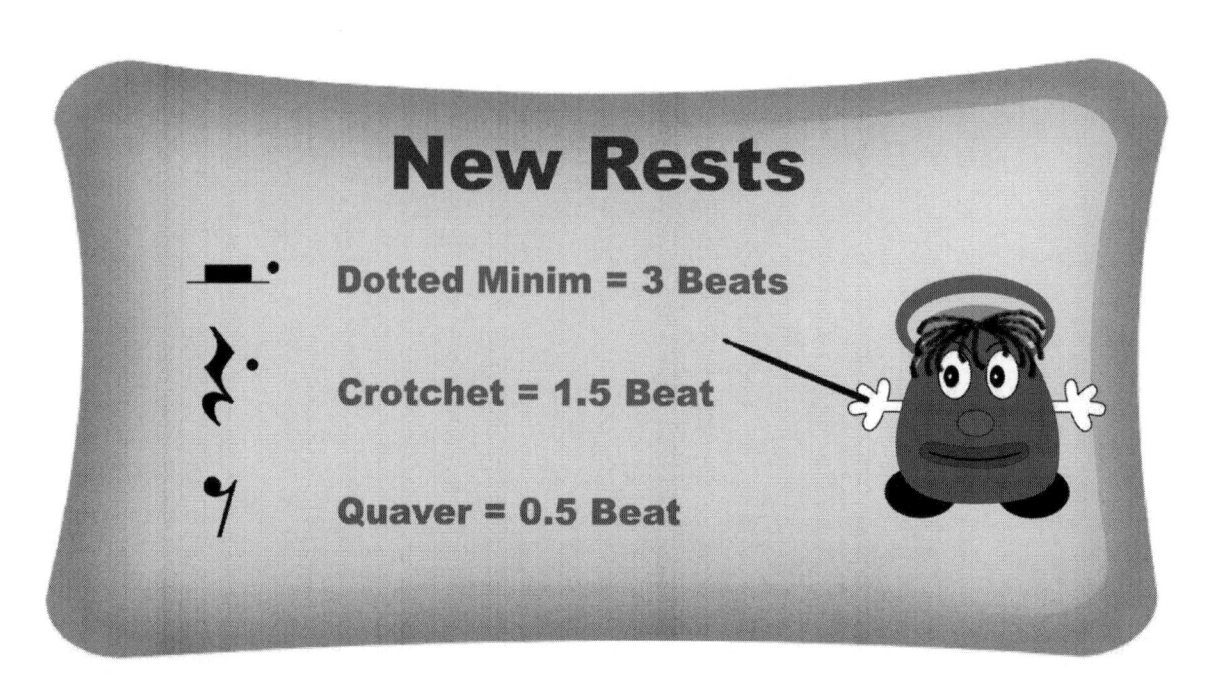

New Rests

- Dotted Minim = 3 Beats
- Crotchet = 1.5 Beat
- Quaver = 0.5 Beat

Tied Notes

Sometimes notes need to be extended and held across a beat or into another bar, and when this happens we use 'tied notes' which means that only the first note is played, but is held for the time length of both notes.

Tied Notes

Only the first note is played when notes are tied together!

"So if two tied crotchets equals a minim, why not just write it as a minim? There doesn't seem much point to having tied notes!"

Yes, I can understand why you are a little confused Gonkling, but ties are only used when the total value of the note or notes held goes across a bar line or sometimes across a beat. Remember you can't have five beats in a **4/4** bar and you can't have any 'leftovers'. But if you like, a tied note is a way of 'carrying over' to the next bar.

I will be showing examples of how these occur shortly, but right now we'll look at a few more time signatures.

The time signature is always shown at the beginning of each piece. And so far we've only really dealt with **4/4** (four crotchets to a bar).

Now we'll look at:

- **2/4**
- **3/4** and
- **6/8**

4/4 Timing

Firstly though, we'll just re-cap the **4/4** timing with quavers included.

4/4 Timing Example

Count evenly and clap on the stars

Remember for this timing we count **1 - 2 - 3 - 4** etc. for each bar, each beat being a crotchet. But if we add quavers, they come in-between these beats so we need to count **1 & 2 & 3 & 4 & 1 & 2 & 3 & 4 &** etc. And an accent should generally be given to the first and third beats.

The last bar of the example above is perhaps a little tricky at first, as two of the crotchets come on the '&' beats. This is known as syncopation and is very common in rag time, jazz and funk music.

2/4 Timing

2/4, as I mentioned only a short while ago, means that there are two quarter notes (crotchets) to each bar. And this is just like 'marching' time. So when counting as we have done previously, you need to count **1 - 2 - 1 - 2** etc.

That's the timing for the crotchets. But if there are quavers involved (which there usually will be) we need to count **1 & 2 & 1 & 2 &** etc. And accent should be given to both first and second beats.

2/4 Timing Example

Count evenly and clap on the stars

Just about all military music is written in **2/4** timing. If you've ever seen the Queens 'Trooping the Colour', you will have heard many!

But **2/4** timing is extensively used in all types of music, including folk and classical.

3/4/ Timing

3/4 timing is Waltz timing and should be counted: **1 - 2 - 3 - 1 - 2 - 3** etc., or if there are quavers involved: **1 & 2 & 3 & 1 & 2 & 3 &** etc., with accent on the first beat.

6/8 Timing

6/8 is different. This means that there are six eighth notes (quavers) to each bar, and these are always two groups of three quavers. So for this you will need to count: **1 - 2 - 3 - 2 - 2 - 3, 1 - 2 - 3 - 2 - 2 - 3** etc. At first to may think that this is similar to **3/4**, but it's not, as the quavers in 3/4 would be three sets of two rather than two sets of three. If this sounds too confusing Gonklings, don't worry about it.

Learn to Play Piano / Keyboard With Filo & Pastry - Copyright © Martin Woodward 2013 - www.gonkmusic.com

All sorts of music is written in **6/8** timing including many jigs, jazz, funk etc., and even ballads (when the tempo is slower).

We have now covered just about all of the most common time signatures. There are others, but having learnt these, you will find little trouble with any *standard* less common ones.

Well that's it from me for now Gonklings, so I'll now hand you back over to Alan Duvet for the rest of the course.

"Thank you Leeroy!"

More Tunes & Exercises

Hello again Gonklings.

I hope that Leeroy has explained the last rhythm section clearly.

Now that we have learnt quavers and new time signatures, the way is clear to begin some new and more interesting tunes and exercises.

But firstly I need to tell you about a few more musical terms and symbols that you will be coming across shortly, and also a little bit about intervals.

Staccato

Previously I have shown you the most usual way of playing the notes whereby you press the second key *as* you are releasing the first thereby creating a smooth transition which is known as **'legato'**. I hope that you have been practicing this correctly and not just banging the keys indiscriminately.

But some notes need to be struck deliberately quickly and sharply. This is known as 'staccato'.

Notes that should be played this way have a dot over or under them as shown here:

"So a dot over a note means it should be played staccato and if the dot is after it means that half as much again should be added to the time length - Yes?"

Absolutely correct Gonkling - well done!

Fermata

The 'Fermata' symbol as shown below indicates a 'pause'.

You will be seeing this in a piece that follows called 'The Clowns Waltz', where there are a lot of pauses when the clowns keep tripping over!

Repeat Bars

As you progress through the new pieces you will come across some 'repeat bars'.

This one means that the whole piece should be repeated from the beginning.

This one means that the bar (or bars) between the markers should be repeated.

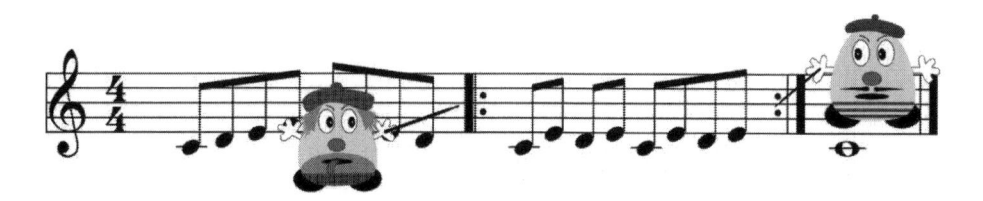

And this one means that the piece should be repeated from the beginning, with the bar marked '1' the first time and the one marked '2' the second time.

There are many more symbols and words that you may need to know in the future, but right now I'm trying to limit this to the minimum so as not to strain your brains any more than necessary.

But, without doubt the most important thing is actual practice on the keyboard. Hopefully, you can manage this at least once a day. But if you can do it twice a day then this is much better. Three times a day would be magnificent and well worth the effort!

"We practice for 30 minutes twice a day!"

Well that's just perfect Gonklings!

Sharps, Flats and Intervals

Right Gonklings I know that you are eager to start learning the black notes, so now we will begin. But firstly you need to learn just a little about 'intervals'.

Now we learnt earlier that the interval from one C to the next is an octave. And indeed this is the same interval from B - B or G - G etc.

Now the smallest interval in Western music is a semitone and that is the interval from any note on the keyboard to its nearest neighbour be it black or white.

So the interval between C and B is a semitone, and also the interval between E and F as in both cases there are no black notes in-between. In all the other cases there *is* a black note in-between, so the semitone interval will be to the black note above or below. And as you can see by the diagram below the black note after C is called C sharp *or* D flat.

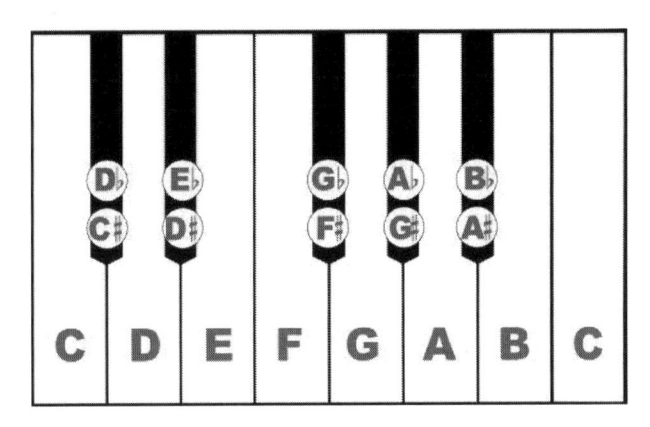

Sharps are always above and flats are always below. See the Sharp, flat and natural symbols below.

♯ Sharp   ♭ Flat   ♮ Natural

Now the interval between C and D is a tone (two semitones) as there is a black note in-between. And the interval between F sharp and G sharp is also a tone, as there is a white note in-between. And the interval between E and F sharp is also a tone as in this case there is a white note in-between.

There are many more bigger intervals that you will need to learn later, but these are only combinations of more tones and semitones and can wait for the time being.

Now sharps and flats occur in music in two different ways:

    a) as accidentals or

b) with key signatures' (which could also include accidentals)

When they are accidentals, they are simply added to the music as and where they occur as shown below.

In this case any repeats of notes that are 'sharpened' or 'flattened' this way remains so for the duration of the bar unless 'naturalised' using the 'natural' symbol.

If you look carefully at the last diagram you will see that both bars are identical, but one has used F sharp and the other has used G flat to produce the same result.

"Why do the black notes have two names? Why not just call them flats or sharps but not both?"

Yes, I can see the confusion Gonklings, but this is because there are flat keys and sharp keys which we'll be learning a little bit about next.

Now everything that we have done so far has been in the key of C major, which is the only major key without any sharps or flats and therefore has no 'key signature'.

As I just mentioned there are two types of keys; flat keys and sharp keys.

The first sharp key you will learn is G major which has one sharp - which is F sharp. You can see the key signature for G major below (left) where it shows the F sharp before the time signature. This means that every time an 'F' occurs in the music - F sharp should be played unless there is a natural sign before it.

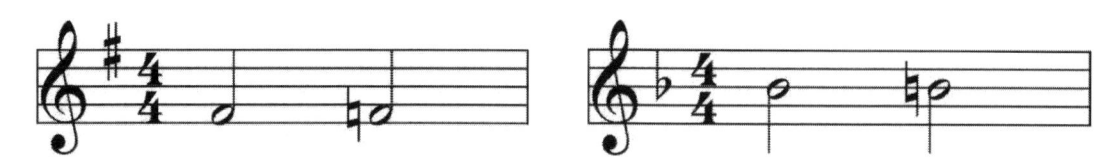

The first flat key that you will learn is F major and this has a B flat and the key signature for this is shown above to the right.

We will be learning more about these two keys and their scales a little later.

The Gonk March

This short easy staccato piece is in **2/4** timing and only requires three fingers and three notes in each hand. You should be able to play this very easily.

Remember to count **1 & 2 & 1 & 2 &** etc.

Most of the notes are straight crotchets, but except for the quavers when you sing **'am a'** and the very last note in the right hand which is a minim and should be held for two beats. ♫ http://gonkmusic.com/gonk_march.html

Learn to Play Piano / Keyboard With Filo & Pastry - Copyright © Martin Woodward 2013 - www.gonkmusic.com

Grubby Hands

This next piece Gonklings was written especially for you, so take special notice.

"*A song written especially for us? M. Duvet you are so very thoughtful!*"

Well you haven't seen it yet!

Although this is simple to play, it is the most difficult piece so far.

Notice that there is a low 'G' in the right hand which is way below the treble clef staff lines and has two ledger lines above it. This is in the fifth bar and is not difficult once you know that it's there.

The left hand will almost certainly need to be practiced separately at first as it is far busier than you are used to and at the end plays two notes together.

The right hand starts with the second finger on C leaving the way clear to use the thumb on the B and lower G.

Singing along as you play will make it easier, and may even get the point across!

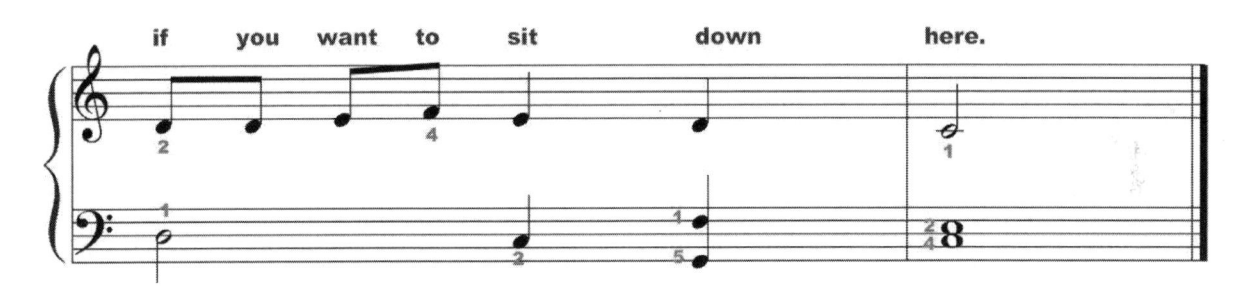

Lyrics:

Don't you forget to wash your grubby little hands if you want to sit at the Key Board. Wash off the marmalade and mud & slime & frogs spawn if you want to sit down here.

"Hmmm!"

♪ http://gonkmusic.com/grubby_hands.html

Learn to Play Piano / Keyboard With Filo & Pastry - Copyright © Martin Woodward 2013 - www.gonkmusic.com

Disaster Strikes

I am afraid Gonklings, that I have some terrible news, just when everything seemed to be going so well.

Angus McDangle has done a runner, probably gone hunting for Wee Yin (Wild Hagis), as it is the start of the Wee Yin hunting season. And worse than that, he has also taken with him the keys to the note cupboard. And if that's not bad enough, Leeroy has gone off on a gig somewhere with his band 'The Grasshoppers', leaving me all on my lonesome.

I am at my wits end, - I just don't know what to do. I have been to the Gonk recruitment agency and all they can come up with is a sooty chimney sweep, a Viking with an enormous chopper ..... and a China Gonk who cannot speak Engilish - or French.

Here they are, see what you think!

No doubt you can see the dilemma that I am having! I guess that you can see which one is which by the way!

"I like the Viking," - says Pastry *"He looks like he could be fun!"*.

"I like the chimney sweep," - says Filo *"He looks even more messy than us!"*

Anyway, after careful consideration, I've decided to employ the China Gonk as my new helper, he might not be much use but at least he can knock up a good stir fry! - And I could not be doing with soot all over my keyboard as well as marmalade and decomposing frogspawn! Or having my hands chopped off by accident!

So here we are, meet Phuket Wong.

Now let me make this very clear, his name is pronounced Pookette! - just like the Island of Phuket in Thailand.

Phuket actually comes from Bangkok in Thailand, so he is not really Chinese, but near enough!

I've spent a full day training him and trying to get him to communicate in English, but my goodness it is hard going. And I have to say that my patience has been stretched to the limit and beyond!

So as Angus McDangle is no longer here and the note cupboard is locked, I am unable to show you anymore of his note charts, although fortunately I do have enough notes for our needs. I have to say that I am really embarrassed about this. I know it's so unprofessional, but what can I do? - it is beyond my control!

But by now, you should know most of the notes and on just about all of the pieces to follow, you will need all of your fingers on both hands.

Anyway hopefully we'll now move on to our next little piece which is the Jolly Farmer. I've left Phuket to stick all the notes in place, so let's see how he has got on.

The Jolly Farmer

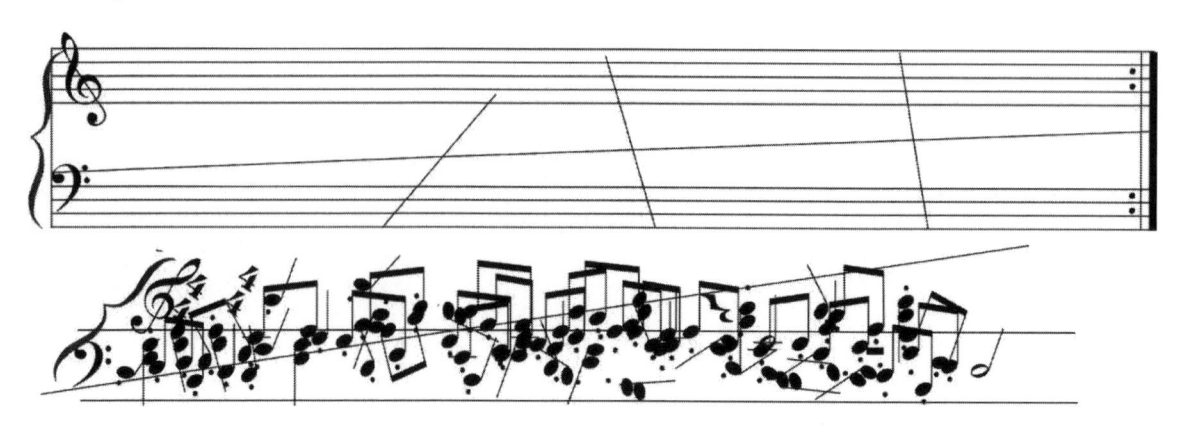

What the ...... for goodness sake - PHUKET! Where are you?

"Sorry, sorry Mr Alan - don't worry I fix it, I fix it! It not me, it fripping plitstick, it not sticking!"

Oh for ff goodness sake, did you try taking the 'fripping' lid off?

"Sorry, sorry Mr Alan - please no hit me, I go to Bangkok!"

You won't have to bother Phuket, I'll do it for you!

"Now's a good time to let the frog loose!" - says Filo in hysterics!"

"Calm down, calm down - Peace be upon you Gonklings!"

Who the heck are you?

"I'm Angelico the Gonk Guardian Angel, and I've come to calm things down! .... Take deep breaths and think happy thoughts!"

Happy thoughts, happy thoughts? ....Well I suppose it was his first day!

"Thank you Mr Alan, thank you. I make you velly nice wok up for tea!"

The Jolly Farmer - Attempt 2

Well what a day we've had eh? But anyway it all ended ok, we got the 'fripping plitstick' working right and everything is fixed, and then we a had a wonderful wok up with oodles of noodles!

Anyway this next little 'staccato' piece is quite simple, especially if you have been practicing the 5 finger exercises from earlier.

The only new thing is that you'll notice that the left hand plays a couple of notes together. This is nowhere as difficult as it looks, as it is mostly repeats.

But you may find it necessary to practice each hand separately at first, which is fine. And of course don't go any faster than you can manage.

♫ http://gonkmusic.com/jolly_farmer_2.html

Learn to Play Piano / Keyboard With Filo & Pastry - Copyright © Martin Woodward 2013 - www.gonkmusic.com

Jolly Milkmaid

This little piece is in **3/4** timing and should be played teasingly and joyfully and mostly staccato. But steady at first, one hand at a time if necessary.

Most importantly notice that the left hand uses the **treble clef** the same as the right hand. There are also repeat marks at the end.

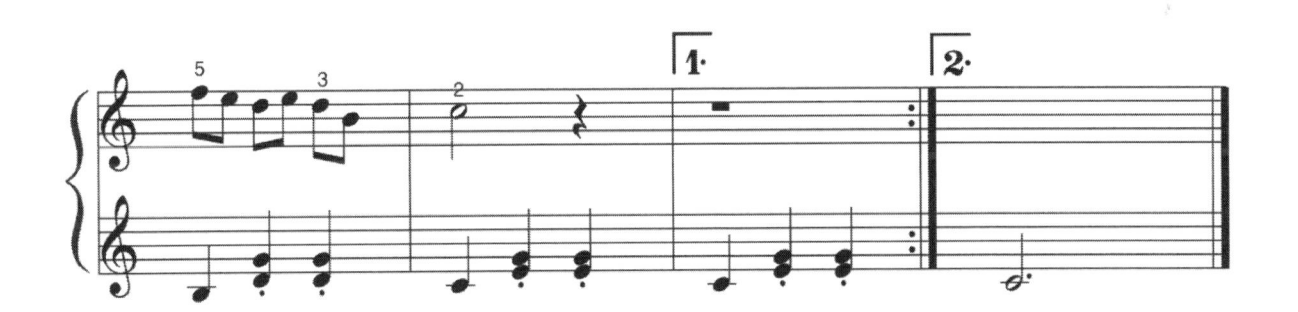

♫ http://gonkmusic.com/jolly_milkmaid.html

Ringo's Beetle Jig

This little piece is fun and a great finger exercise. And actually by playing this you will also be playing some diatonic broken chords, which you'll be learning at a later date. ♫ http://gonkmusic.com/ringos_jig.html

Notice the 'Da Capo Al Fine' message at the end. This means that the piece ends at the 'Fine' sign (at the end of the 4th bar) after the repeats.

If you want to sing along, the singing starts just after the 'Fine' sign and the repeated first 4 bars are instrumental.

Note that the fingering changes on the repeated notes to prepare for what follows.

Do not play this any faster than you can manage 'in time'.

Ringo's Beetle Jig (words)

I am a Black Beetle my name is Ringo
It's Saturday night and I'm off to the Bingo
You can come too if you know how to play
But please don't expect me to pay!

And after the Bingo we'll probly go dancin'
With having six legs it's extremely enhancin'
And then when we're done, we'll all go to bed
And hopefully wake up in the morning!

And then on Sunday we'll all go to church
to pray for forgiveness for all of our sins
For me it takes longest, I'll not tell you why
But pray that I'll still go to heaven!

And after our prayers we'll all dig the garden
And make sure the flowers are watered and fed
And then we'll just rest and re-charge our batteries
in time for the next week ahead!

So this is the story of Ringo the Beetle
I hope I've not bored you or got on your wick
but please be assured that it's only a song
that thankfully dunt last too long!

The Clown Waltz

While playing this fun little piece you need to think 'Clowns'! Imagine a Clown Ball where all the clowns are waltzing and tripping over one another - hence the several pauses.

This should be played 'lightly' - almost staccato.

Notice in the 18th bar and a few beyond there appears to be a dotted minim followed by a minim (making 5 beats which of course doesn't compute). But the dotted minim is held for all 3 beats and the following minim added for beats 2 and 3. ♪ http://gonkmusic.com/clown_waltz.html

Two More finger exercises

Here's a couple more really useful finger exercises.

I haven't included any fingering with this first one, as the right hand simply starts with the thumb then moves up in order.

And the same for the left hand, which starts with the 5th finger and moves up in order.

This exercise is particularly useful as an aid to strengthening your 4th and 5th fingers, which by nature are the weakest. But don't overdo it, if your fingers start hurting, give it a rest! ♫ http://gonkmusic.com/more_finger_ex.html

Notice with this next exercise that there is a gap of a third at the beginning of each measure, which enables the piece to ascend the scale before descending in a similar way.

Practice this one hand at a time before trying both hands together.

Your Second Test

Question 1

Looking at the keyboard chart shown here:

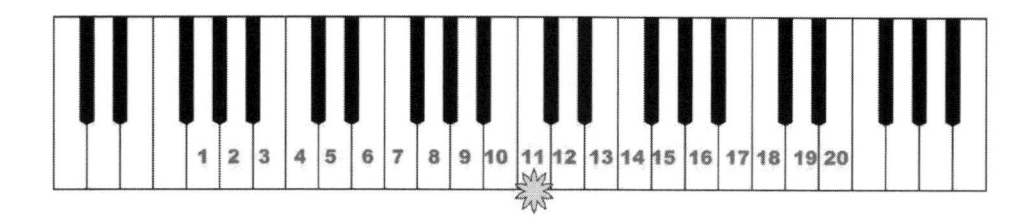

What are the notes called that are numbered:

a) 1?

b) 20?

c) 8?

d) 6?

e) 16?

Question 2

Looking at the following diagram which is in the **treble** clef:

State the names of each note in order.

Question 3

Looking at the following diagram which is in the **bass** clef:

As before, state the notes in order.

Question 4

How many quavers equals a dotted crotchet?

Question 5

How many quavers equals a semibreve?

Question 6

Is the interval from A up to B a tone or a semitone?

Question 7

Is the interval from F down to E a tone or a semitone?

Question 8

How many quavers could there be in a **6/8** bar?

Question 9

How many quavers could there be in a **4/4** bar?

Question 10

Out of the following numbers, which is the odd one out and why?

1, 6, 9, 10, 11, 14 & 20.

Your First Scales

Pre Scale Exercises

Up to now Gonklings, none of the exercises or tunes that we have covered require any finger crossovers.

But in order to play scales and more interesting pieces finger crossovers are essential.

The most common crossovers are achieved by passing the thumb under the third or fourth fingers ascending and passing the third or fourth fingers over the thumb when descending, as shown in the following photos.

Passing the Thumb under (ascending)

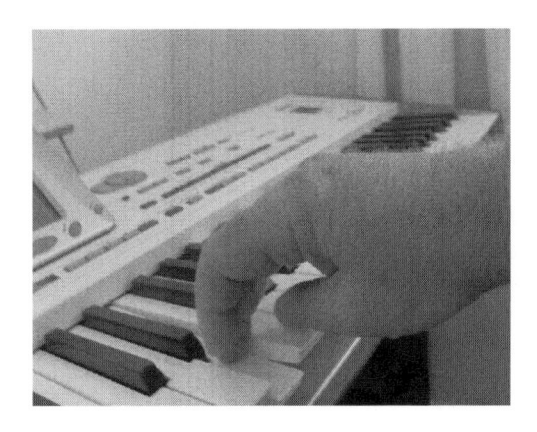

Passing the 3rd Finger over (descending)

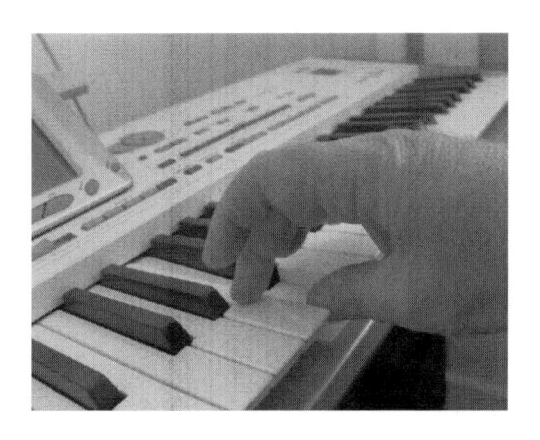

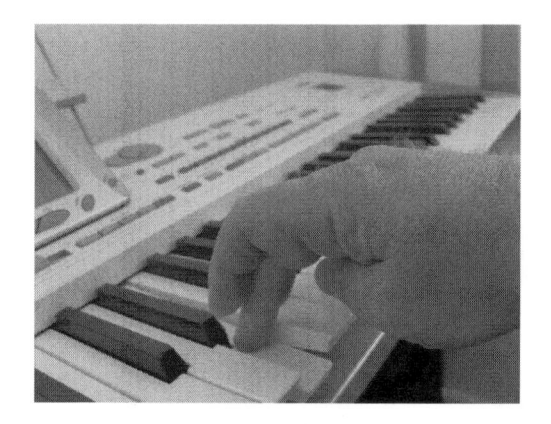

In order to help you learn this technique, I have included this next exercise, but **you must** follow the fingering as stated so that you can practice the finger crossovers.

Practice this slowly and evenly. ♪ http://gonkmusic.com/pre_scale.html

"Excuse me M. Duvet, but what exactly is a scale?"

A scale is a series of notes played in order usually ascending and then descending for one or more octaves.

There are different types of scales including:

- Major
- Minor (harmonic and melodic)
- Chromatic
- Blues
- Pentatonic (major and minor)
- Whole tone

What identifies the different types of scales is the intervals used in their makeup. However, we will only be dealing with a few major scales, harmonic minor scales and the chromatic scale in this book.

To explain further we'll firstly look at the C major scale.

C Major Scale

Now Gonklings, the next diagram shows the C major scale for two octaves.

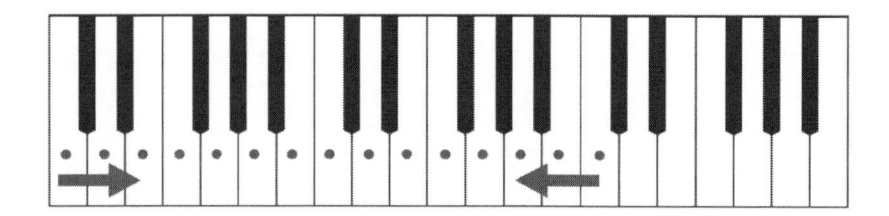

If you remember what I said previously about intervals and look carefully at the diagram you'll see that the intervals are as follows:

1. C - D is a tone
2. D - E is a tone
3. E - F is a semi-tone
4. F - G is a tone
5. G - A is a tone
6. A - B is a tone
7. B - C is a semi-tone

Or to put it another way it's T - T - S - T - T - T - S for a one octave span.

Here's the notation for the C major scale ascending and descending for two octaves. Notice that there are finger crossovers from E - F and B - C in the right hand and from G - A and C - D in the left hand.

Notice also that the left hand changes clefs from bass to treble and back.

G Major Scale

Now, if we use the same pattern of intervals T - T - S - T - T - T - S and begin on the note G we will get the G major scale as shown below.

But in this case interval sequence has forced an F sharp as shown in the key signature.

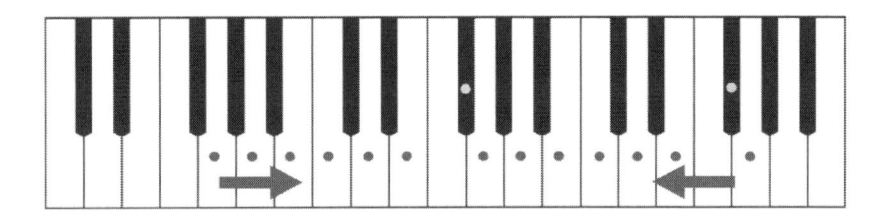

The fingering for this is exactly the same as the C major scale and in fact this is the case for all of the major and minor scales which begin on a white note with the exception of F major and F minor. The reason for this will become clear when I show you the F major scale shortly.

Notice here that the scale begins and ends with the right hand on the G below middle C which we've seen previously.

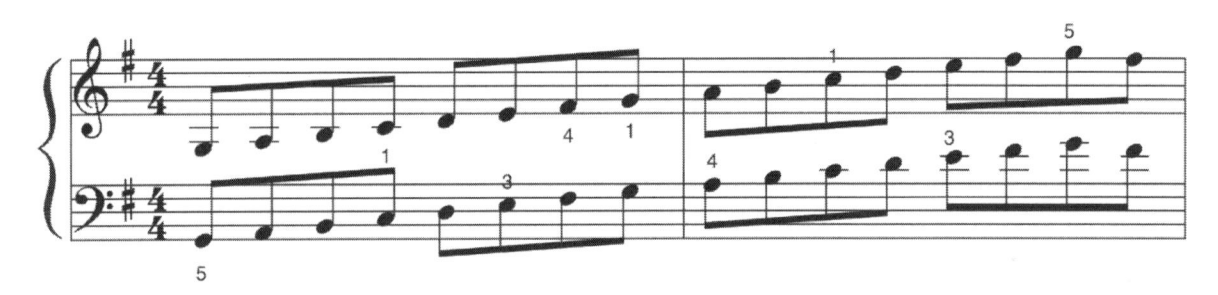

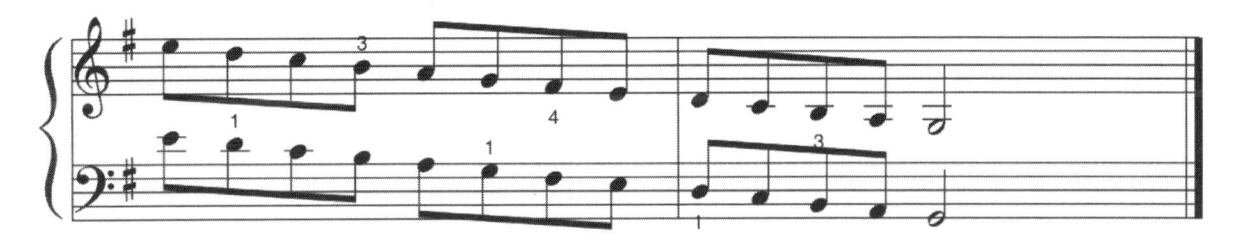

All of the scales incidentally, should be practiced with each hand separately and then together at a speed which you are comfortable with. Having learnt the fingering and sharps, you should not need to read the music to practice any scale exercise.

Always pay attention to even timing and correct hand positioning.

F Major Scale

Starting the same interval sequence T - T - S - T - T - T - S on F will achieve the F major scale which contains B flat (as shown in the key signature).

If you look at the keyboard diagram below you'll notice that the fourth note is B flat, so if we used the same fingering as the other scales 123,1234 you will notice that this will involve passing the thumb under the third finger onto B flat which is frankly stupid.

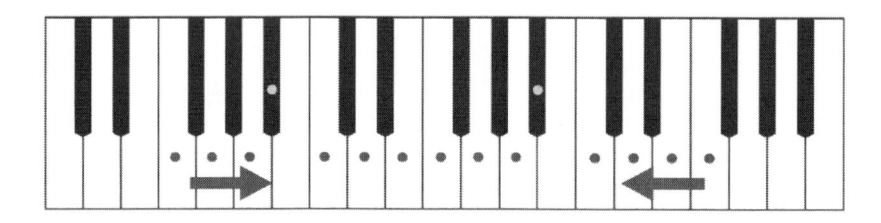

So as an alternative for this scale we use the fingering 1234,123 as shown below and therefore using the fourth finger on the B flat which works well.

Notice that the right hand starts on the F below middle C which has three ledger lines, but this is not hard to read as each note comes in order, but remember the B flat!

Needless to say Gonklings, practice this slowly at your own pace and in your own time, one hand at a time and then both hands together.

Using the same sequence of intervals T - T - S - T - T - T - S see if you can work out what the D major scale will be.

Learn to Play Piano / Keyboard With Filo & Pastry - Copyright © Martin Woodward 2013 - www.gonkmusic.com

Chromatic Scale

The chromatic scale is one on its own and is shown here starting and finishing on C for two octaves.

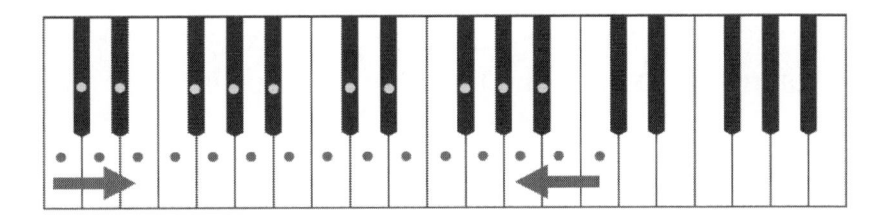

Ideally this scale should be practiced for two or more octaves starting on various notes.

Although the (one octave) notation below looks complicated, in fact it's not.

As each note is played one after the other, no reading ability is required to play this scale other than perhaps when you first learn the fingering.

Big Gonk Tip! - The trick to learning this easily is to remember where the 2nd finger goes - F and C in the right hand and E and B in the left hand.

♫ http://gonkmusic.com/scales_2.html

"So what about minor scales?"

There are two types of minor scales - *harmonic* and *melodic*. We will deal with the first few harmonic minor scales next.

The Harmonic Minor Scale

Each major key has a relative minor which shares the same key signature as the major key.

The relative minor can always be found by counting three semitones down from the first note (the tonic) of the major scale. For instance three semitones down from C is A, therefore A minor is the relative to C major. Similarly E minor is the relative to G major and D minor the relative to F major and these are the three harmonic minor scales which we will be dealing with here.

Now Gonklings, although the minor keys share the same key signature as their relative major keys, each minor key has one or more additional sharp(s) and these are always shown as accidentals as and when they occur (never in the key signature). In the harmonic minor scale, there will only ever be one (extra) sharp, which is always one semitone down from the tonic (the first and last note of the scale).

"So what is the difference between a major scale and a minor scale?"

Well Gonklings, the difference is caused because of the different intervals. If you've been paying attention you should know that the interval sequence for all major scales is: T - T - S - T - T - T - S.

There are two conventional minor scales, the 'harmonic' and the 'melodic', both of which have different interval sequences. Here we will only be dealing with the 'harmonic' minor scale which is the most common.

If you look carefully at the keyboard diagrams that follow you will see that the interval sequence for this scale is: T - S - T - T - S - (T + S) - S.

And if you compare this sequence to the major scale you'll see that the difference is that both the third and sixth notes are flattened by a semitone. But I must stress Gonklings, that it's not essential that you understand all this at this stage.

The only important things are for you to learn to play the scales correctly at your own speed and listen to the differences in how they sound.

All of the scales shown here are on the same link, so you can easily compare them and hear how they sound.

Here's the link again - ♪ http://gonkmusic.com/scales_2.html

Learn to Play Piano / Keyboard With Filo & Pastry - Copyright © Martin Woodward 2013 - www.gonkmusic.com

A Minor (Harmonic) Scale

Ok Gonklings, so our first harmonic minor scale is A minor as shown below.

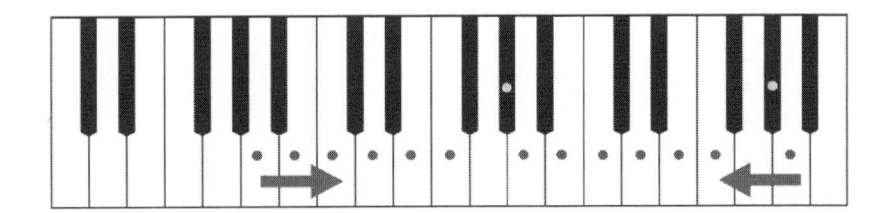

So as A minor is the relative to C major, there is no key signature, but as you will see the T - S - T - T - S - (T + S) - S sequence has forced a G# which has been included in the notation (below) with an accidental sharp.

Notice in the second bar there is no accidental sharp indicated for the second G#, but remember that once an accidental has been used it remains so for the rest of the bar unless cancelled by using the 'natural' symbol as shown previously - so it's still a G#!

The fingering is exactly the same as the C major scale which is 123,1234 for the right hand and 54321,321 for the left hand, although I've only included the important fingering in the notation below.

Notice also the treble clef in the left hand again.

"I find it hard stretching the interval from the F to the G# with my right hand" - says Pastry.

Yes Gonkling, at first this is a bit of a stretch between the third and fourth fingers, but as you practice, this will become very easy.

Learn to Play Piano / Keyboard With Filo & Pastry - Copyright © Martin Woodward 2013 - www.gonkmusic.com

E Minor (Harmonic) Scale

The relative minor to G major is E minor, which is our next harmonic minor scale as shown below.

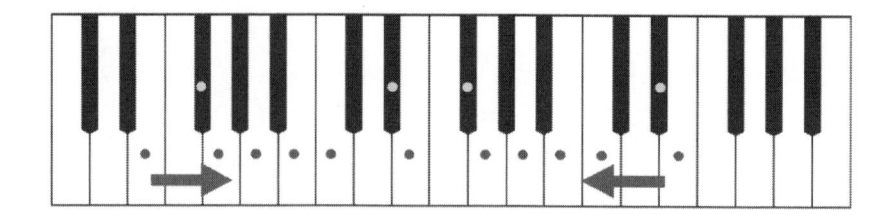

As G major has an F# in the key signature, so does E minor, although the interval sequence T - S - T - T - S - (T + S) - S has forced the D# as well which is added as an accidental.

The fingering is exactly the same for both hands as all of the other scales dealt with, with the exception of F major.

The notation might look a little frightening, as the top E is way above treble clef stave and has three ledger lines. But remember that the second octave where this occurs is only a direct copy of the first, but an octave higher. So actually very little 'reading' is required for any of the scales once they are learnt.

And as with the A minor scale, note that the accidental D# is only shown once in the second bar, but the second D is still a D#!

D Minor (Harmonic) Scale

Our final harmonic minor scale is D minor, the relative to F major and therefore has a B^b in the key signature as well as the accidental C#s.

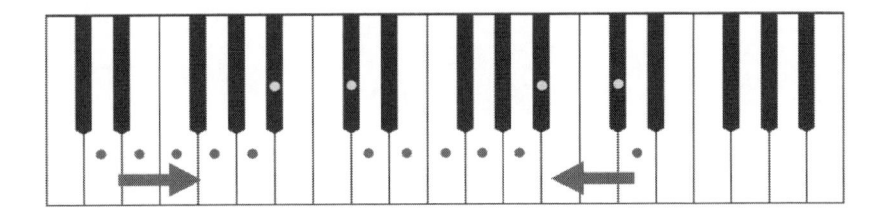

"So if this is a 'flat' key, how come there is an accidental 'sharp' and not an accidental flat?" - says Filo.

Yes Gonkling this is a logical question, but with all the minor scales regardless of flat or sharp keys, this sometimes does happen. And there could also be an accidental flat in a sharp key although this never occurs in the scales.

The fingering again is the same as the others (except F major), but the stretch between the third and fourth fingers from the B^b to the C# might be a bit tricky to start with, but after a little practice will become easy.

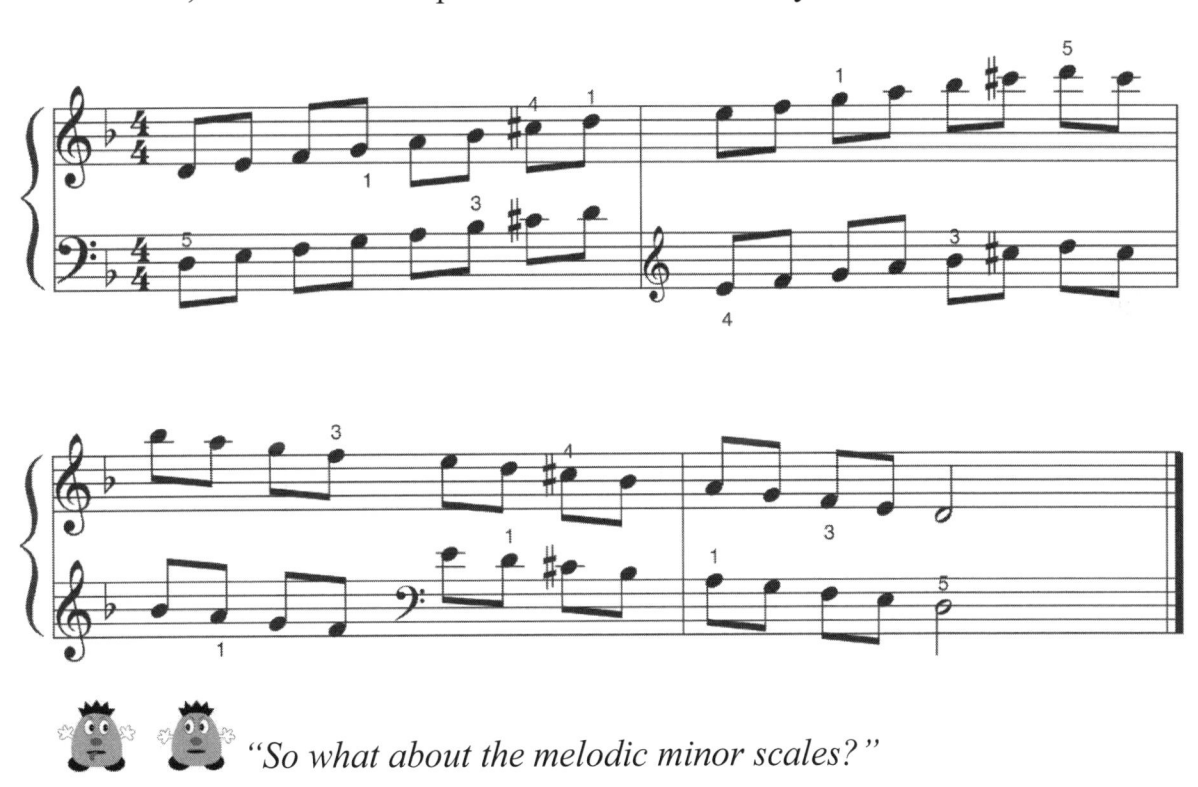

"So what about the melodic minor scales?"

We're not going to deal with this scale here Gonklings, but in brief the melodic minor scales ascend with a sharpened 6th and 7th, but descend with a natural 6th and 7th.

An example can be seen here: http://learn-keyboard.co.uk/scale_box.html .

Test Answers

Don't forget Gonklings, if you have answered any questions incorrectly it only means that you have to go back and review what you didn't understand.

Test 1 Answers

1. a) C, b) F, c) A, d) D, e) E.

2. a) C - 11, b) D - 19, c) F - 14, d) D - 12, e) B - 17.

3. a) C - 11, b) D - 12, c) A - 4, d) C - 6, e) E - 8.

4. Two crotchets = a minim.

5. Four crotchets = a semibreve.

6. Crotchet.

7. Semibreve.

8. Crotchet.

9. There could only be two minims in a **4/4** bar.

10. Pastry has the frog in his pocket.

Test 2 Answers

1. a) G, b) E, c) G, d) E, e) A.

2. a) B, b) C, c) A, d) C sharp, e) E flat.

3. a) C, b) A, c) D flat, d) B, e) F sharp.

4. Three quavers = a dotted crotchet.

5. Eight quavers = a semibreve.

6. A to B is a tone.

7. F to E is a semitone.

8. There could be six quavers in a **6/8** bar.

9. There could be eight quavers in a **4/4** bar.

10. 20 of course is odd one out, as it only one where lice or chips not included!

"Whoopee doo, we have passed both our tests with Gonk Honours!"

Sad Goodbyes & Download Link

Well Gonklings the time has come to say our sad goodbyes!

I say this with a lump in my throat and a tear in my eye, as I have so enjoyed being your tutor for this course. I do hope that you have enjoyed it as much as me.

And if you have, I would really appreciate it if you'd give me some positive feedback, as even a fully grown Gonk like me needs a bit of encouragement now and again.

If this book is well received, then Book 2 will follow shortly with many more new tunes and exercises and also much more about scales, chords and arpeggios. But hopefully, you have enough to be going on with for the time being.

If you would like the printable pdf version of this book, this is available to you from our website at http://gonkmusic.com/learn_with_filo_dl.html at no extra cost. If you are copying this link be sure to include the underscores between the words!

You will have to sign in and log on, but this is just to prevent fraud.

If you have any trouble with this or if you have any questions about this book, I can be contacted via the website http://gonkmusic.com 'contact' page. Be sure to address you queries to me - Alan Duvet!

Finally, I would like to extend my sincere thanks to Angus McDangle (wherever he has scuttled off to); Leeroy; Phuket Wong; my resident students Filo and Pastry;

and most importantly to **YOU** for trusting me and buying this book - **Thank You Sincerely!**

Learn to Play Piano / Keyboard With Filo & Pastry - Copyright © Martin Woodward 2013 - www.gonkmusic.com

Further Reading

You may also perhaps be interested in some of the following books, the details for which can all be seen on my websites at http://gonkmuisc.com and http://learn-keyboard.co.uk .

- Learn How to Play Electronic Keyboard or Piano In a Week!
- New Easy Original Piano / Keyboard Music - Beginners - Intermediate
- Keyboard / Piano Improvisation One Note At a Time - Learn to Improvise from Scratch!
- Learn Keyboard / Piano Scales & Arpeggios In Music Notation & Keyboard View!
- Piano / Keyboard Chords - In Keyboard View Including 9ths and 13ths Etc.

You may also find the following web page useful - http://www.learn-keyboard.co.uk/musical_terms.html . If copying the links be sure to include the underscores between the words.

Printed in Great Britain
by Amazon.co.uk, Ltd.,
Marston Gate.